וְזֹאת הַתּוֹרָה עֵץ חַיִּים הִיא

וְזֹאת הַתּוֹרָה

What's the most recent honor you received that made you proud? Maybe it was a diploma, or a pennant from the county softball tournament, or a trophy for best project at the science fair. You might have held up your diploma for everyone to see, or taken a team photo with the pennant, or polished your trophy until it sparkled!

The Jewish people are proud of the Torah, and each time after it is read, we lift it up high so the congregation can see the inside of the scroll. The honor of lifting up the Torah is called *hagbahah*. We proudly raise the Torah to show symbolically that the words we just read aloud are the same words that Moses spoke to the Israelites in the wilderness almost 3,500 years ago.

Practice reading וְזֹאת הַתּוֹרָה aloud.

1. וְזֹאת הַתּוֹרָה אֲשֶׁר־שָׂם מֹשֶׁה לִפְנֵי בְּנֵי יִשְׂרָאֵל,
2. עַל־פִּי יְיָ בְּיַד־מֹשֶׁה.

And this is the Torah that Moses placed before the people of Israel,
by the word of Adonai through Moses.

וְזֹאת

and this is

שָׁם

placed, put

מֹשֶׁה

Moses

לִפְנֵי

before

בְּנֵי

people of

יִשְׂרָאֵל

Israel

SEARCH AND CIRCLE

Circle the Hebrew word that means the same as the English.

English			
and this is	וְחַיֵּי עוֹלָם	וְזֹאת	וְנָתַן
placed, put	שָׁם	בָּחַר	עוֹשֶׂה
Moses	מֹשֶׁה	מֶלֶךְ	מִצִּיּוֹן
before	לָנוּ	לִפְנֵי	בָּנוּ
Israel	אֲבוֹתֵינוּ לְעוֹלָם וָעֶד	יִשְׂרָאֵל

We hold the Torah up high for the entire congregation to see.

WHAT'S MISSING?

Fill in the missing Hebrew words to complete the prayer.

וְזֹאת _____ אֲשֶׁר־שָׂם

לִפְנֵי בְּנֵי _____, עַל־פִּי יְיָ

בְּיַד־_____.

2

Prayer Building Blocks

וְזֹאת הַתּוֹרָה **"and this is the Torah"**

וְזֹאת means "and this is."

וְ means _____.

זֹאת means _____.

הַ means _____.

וְזֹאת הַתּוֹרָה means _____.

FROM THE SOURCES

וְזֹאת הַתּוֹרָה is taken from the Torah. Below are three verses from the Torah. Find and underline all the words of וְזֹאת הַתּוֹרָה. (*Remember:* יְ *can also be written* יְהוָֹה.) Practice reading all the lines aloud.

	וְזֹאת הַתּוֹרָה אֲשֶׁר־שָׂם 44
Deuteronomy 4:44-45	45 מֹשֶׁה לִפְנֵי בְּנֵי יִשְׂרָאֵל: אֵלֶּה הָעֵדֹת
	וְהַחֻקִּים וְהַמִּשְׁפָּטִים אֲשֶׁר דִּבֶּר מֹשֶׁה
	אֶל־בְּנֵי יִשְׂרָאֵל בְּצֵאתָם מִמִּצְרָיִם:

Numbers 9:23	23 אֶת־מִשְׁמֶרֶת יְהוָה שָׁמָרוּ עַל־פִּי יְהוָה בְּיַד־
	מֹשֶׁה:

3

אֲשֶׁר־שָׂם מֹשֶׁה "that Moses placed"

שָׂם means "placed" or "put."

מֹשֶׁה means "Moses."

What did Moses place? Write your answer in Hebrew. _____

Read these sentences aloud and underline the Hebrew word for Moses in each one.

וַיְהִי בִּנְסֹעַ הָאָרֹן וַיֹּאמֶר מֹשֶׁה

לֹא קָם בְּיִשְׂרָאֵל כְּמֹשֶׁה עוֹד נָבִיא, וּמַבִּיט אֶת תְּמוּנָתוֹ

בָּרוּךְ אַתָּה יְיָ, הַבּוֹחֵר בַּתּוֹרָה וּבְמֹשֶׁה עַבְדּוֹ...

וּבִנְבִיאֵי הָאֱמֶת וָצֶדֶק

תּוֹרָה צִוָּה לָנוּ מֹשֶׁה, מוֹרָשָׁה קְהִלַּת יַעֲקֹב

לִפְנֵי בְּנֵי יִשְׂרָאֵל "before the people of Israel"

לִפְנֵי means "before."

בְּנֵי יִשְׂרָאֵל means "the people of Israel."

Read the underlined part of this prayer:

וְזֹאת הַתּוֹרָה אֲשֶׁר־שָׂם מֹשֶׁה לִפְנֵי בְּנֵי יִשְׂרָאֵל,

עַל־פִּי יְיָ בְּיַד־מֹשֶׁה.

We translate these words as "by the word of Adonai through Moses."

- Circle the Hebrew word for Adonai in the underlined part of the Hebrew prayer above.
- Put a star above the Hebrew word for Moses.
- Whose words or mitzvot are contained in the Torah?
  Write your answer in Hebrew. _____
- Who brought those words or mitzvot to the people?
  Write your answer in Hebrew. _____

עֵץ חַיִּים הִיא

Before returning the Torah to the Ark, we roll it and dress it again in its cover and ornaments. The honor of rolling and dressing the Torah is called *g'lilah*.

As it is returned to the Ark, we sing עֵץ חַיִּים הִיא, a prayer of rich language and imagery comparing the Torah to a tree of life.

As a tree is a living thing, with roots that reach down into the earth and branches that reach up to the sun, so is the Torah a living thing symbolically. Its roots reach back to our ancestors who first received it and followed its commandments. Its branches are the generations that continue to read it and believe in its teachings. By carrying on the tradition of reading and studying Torah, and by passing that tradition on to future generations, we strengthen our roots and allow our Jewish heritage to grow, to flourish, and to live on forever.

Practice reading עֵץ חַיִּים הִיא **aloud.**

1. עֵץ־חַיִּים הִיא לַמַּחֲזִיקִים בָּהּ, וְתֹמְכֶיהָ מְאֻשָּׁר.
2. דְּרָכֶיהָ דַרְכֵי־נֹעַם, וְכָל־נְתִיבוֹתֶיהָ שָׁלוֹם.

It (the Torah) is a tree of life to those who uphold it, and those who support it are happy. Its ways are ways of pleasantness and all its paths are peace.

PRAYER DICTIONARY

עֵץ

tree

חַיִּים

(of) life

מְאֻשָּׁר

happy

דְּרָכֶיהָ

its ways

דַּרְכֵי

ways of

נֹעַם

pleasantness

שָׁלוֹם

peace

MATCH GAME

Connect each Hebrew word to its English meaning.

pleasantness	עֵץ
its ways	מְאֻשָּׁר
ways of	דְּרָכֶיהָ
happy	דַּרְכֵי
tree	נֹעַם

This rabbi and cantor roll the Torah before dressing it and returning it to the Ark.

DESCRIPTIVE WORDS

Fill in the English meanings for the Hebrew words describing the Torah.

חַיִּים   _____

מְאֻשָּׁר   _____

נֹעַם   _____

שָׁלוֹם   _____

Prayer Building Blocks

עֵץ חַיִּים הִיא לַמַּחֲזִיקִים בָּהּ

"it is a tree of life to those who uphold it"

עֵץ means _____.

חַיִּים means _____.

Why do *you* think the Torah is compared to a tree?

_____

Fill in the missing words in English.

The Torah is a _____ to those who uphold it.

Now fill in the missing words in Hebrew.

_____ הִיא לַמַּחֲזִיקִים בָּהּ.

DID YOU KNOW?

The two wooden rollers to which the Torah parchment is attached are also called עֲצֵי חַיִּים (the plural of עֵץ חַיִּים), trees of life.

Why is this an appropriate name for the rollers?

_____

מְאֻשָּׁר "happy"

מְאֻשָּׁר means "happy."

אֹשֶׁר means "happiness."

Read the following lines aloud and circle the words meaning "happy."

אַשְׁרֵי יוֹשְׁבֵי בֵיתֶךָ עוֹד יְהַלְלוּךָ סֶלָה.

אַשְׁרֵי הָעָם שֶׁכָּכָה לּוֹ אַשְׁרֵי הָעָם שֶׁיְיָ אֱלֹהָיו.

How many words did you circle? _____

7

דְּרָכֶיהָ דַרְכֵי נֹעַם **"its ways are ways of pleasantness"**

דְּרָכֶיהָ means "its ways."

דַרְכֵי means "ways of."

Both words are variations of דֶּרֶךְ ("road" or "way"). Circle the three letters
meaning "road" or "way" in the words below.

דְּרָכֶיהָ   דַרְכֵי

Read the two sentences below and circle the words meaning "road" or "way."

1. צַדִּיק יְיָ בְּכָל דְּרָכָיו, וְחָסִיד בְּכָל מַעֲשָׂיו

2. בְּשִׁבְתְּךָ בְּבֵיתֶךָ וּבְלֶכְתְּךָ בַדֶּרֶךְ וּבְשָׁכְבְּךָ וּבְקוּמֶךָ

FROM THE SOURCES

עֵץ חַיִּים הִיא is taken from the תַּנַ"ךְ (Proverbs 3).
Below is the excerpt from Proverbs in which עֵץ חַיִּים הִיא is found.
Underline all the words of the עֵץ חַיִּים הִיא prayer. Then read
the Biblical excerpt.

16 אֹרֶךְ יָמִים בִּימִינָהּ
בִּשְׂמֹאולָהּ עֹשֶׁר וְכָבוֹד:
17 דְּרָכֶיהָ דַרְכֵי־נֹעַם
וְכָל־נְתִיבוֹתֶיהָ שָׁלוֹם:
18 עֵץ־חַיִּים הִיא לַמַּחֲזִיקִים בָּהּ
וְתֹמְכֶיהָ מְאֻשָּׁר:

How does the order of the verses in the תַּנַ"ךְ differ from our version
in the siddur?

_____

Copyright © 2004 by Behrman House, Inc., Springfield, NJ. www.behrmanhouse.com; Author: Terry Kaye; Contributing Authors: Claudia Grossman and Lori Justice; Artist: Ilene Winn-Lederer; Photographs: Creative Image (2, 6). ISBN 0-87441-767-8 (V'zot HaTorah/ Eitz Hayyim Hi); Manufactured in the United States of America.